PRAYERS

to use with Young People

DENHOLM HOUSE PRESS
National Christian Education Council
Robert Denholm House, Nutfield, Redhill,
Surrey RH1 4HW

First published 1976

ISBN 0 85213 147 X

Printed by
JOHN BLACKBURN LIMITED LEEDS

PRAYERS
to use with Young People

£1·45.

Books in this series:

PRAYERS TO USE WITH UNDER-FIVES
PRAYERS TO USE WITH 5–8s
PRAYERS TO USE WITH 8–11s
PRAYERS TO USE WITH YOUNG PEOPLE

In preparation:

PRAYERS TO USE WITH 11–13s

CONTRIBUTORS

The following have contributed prayers to this book:

IVOR H. JONES, MA, FRCO

ANTHONY E. PERRY, MA

A. TREVOR HUBBARD, BA, BD

EDITED BY AUBREY G. SMITH

Cover design by James Moss

ACKNOWLEDGEMENT

The Rev. Anthony E. Perry wishes to acknowledge the help of Mr. W. B. Mountford, Headmaster of Prior's Court School near Newbury, and the boys of the school who wrote a number of prayers which have been included.

CONTENTS

EDITORIAL FOREWORD

This book is one of a Series which aims to provide a wide range of prayers for use with various age-groups.

The prayers are original, having been specially written by people conversant with the needs of children and young people. They are grouped under themes, some of which relate closely to the Christian Year, others to everyday experience. An index is included at the end of the book so that prayers or specific topics can be located more easily. This will be particularly helpful since some topics have a place in more than one section.

The occasions when the books can prove useful are numerous and varied: they include Day School Assemblies and worship times in the classroom, Church Family Worship, Sunday groups and week-night activities. Not least, they may find a place in the home, either read by parents to smaller children or used by older boys and girls themselves in their private devotions.

We hope that teachers, ministers, leaders, parents – and the young people – will find in these books a rich source of prayer material.

1. God our Father

'WE PRAISE YOU, GOD'

We praise you, God all-powerful, for creating the universe, with all its stars and planets, and for making our world, and us who live in it. Your power runs through everything that exists, and you sustain all things, from the furthest galaxy to the smallest atom.

We praise you, God all-loving, because, for all your might and majesty, you care for each individual far more than your stars and planets; and that is what Jesus came to show us.

You are truly great, Lord God: your greatness lies not only in your power to create a universe, but in your willingness to love ordinary people like us.

THE GROUND OF OUR EXISTENCE

Lord God, you are the ground of our existence.
You brought us into being,
you watch over us day by day,
you give meaning to our lives,
you support us in our need.
Lord God, we worship and adore you.

TWO PRAYERS OF CONFESSION

(a)

'Be good to me, God, in your love;
in your mercy blot out my offences.
Wash me clean from all my guilt,
and cleanse me from my sin.
Create a pure heart in me, God,
a new and unwavering spirit.'

(From Psalm 51. 1–2, 10)

(b)

When we are faced with the greatness of your love, and think of ourselves in comparison, we realise, Lord, how far short we fall. Our lives should be a reflection of your love; love should be the basis of our living. But we become more concerned with ourselves than with doing your will, or thinking of others.

(Silence)

Yet in your love for us, Lord, though we sometimes fail, you are always ready to give us a new start. We praise and thank you for that, and ask you to forgive our failures in love, help us begin afresh, and give us a love like yours.

A THANKSGIVING PSALM

The response is: **Rejoice in the Lord, all the earth.**

It is suggested that the leader speaks the response at each point, the young people repeating it after him.

Rejoice in the Lord, all the earth.
Worship him gladly,
sing with joy in his presence.
Rejoice in the Lord, all the earth.

The Lord alone is God.
It is he who has made us, and we are his,
his people, the sheep of his flock.
Rejoice in the Lord, all the earth.

Pass through his gates with thanks,
and into his courts with praise.
Thank him and bless his name.
Rejoice in the Lord, all the earth.

Why? Because God is good,
his love never fails.
He can be trusted, for ever and ever.
Rejoice in the Lord, all the earth.

(From Psalm 100)

THE GLORY OF GOD

Lord God our king,
how glorious is your name throughout the earth!
Your majesty is praised as high as the skies.
When I look at the heavens, the work of your hands,
the moon and the stars you have set in their place,
what is man that you notice him,
mortal man that you care for him?
Yet you have made him little less than a god,
crowning him with glory and honour.
You make him master of all you created,
you put everything under his feet.
Lord God our king,
how glorious is your name throughout the earth!

(Parts of Psalm 8)

THE LOVE OF GOD

'I am convinced that there is nothing – in death or life, or among spiritual powers, in the present or the future, or in forces of any kind – nothing in all creation that can separate us from the love of God in Christ Jesus our Lord.' *(From Romans 8. 38–9)*

Praise be to you, our loving God.

2. God and His Universe

TWO PRAYERS OF THANKSGIVING (written by teenagers)

(a)

Father, thank you for all the colour in our lives:
the fresh green of the leaves in spring,
the drab green of the trees in autumn;
for the oranges and reds of this world,
and the blues and browns;
for the bright dresses of women,
and the colourless suits of men.
Thank you for the white snow-capped mountains,
and the bright blue of the sky.

(b)

Thank you for the miracle of creation. The shaping and forming of things with love and devotion, like a boy making a model or carving wood. Great care is taken, and pride and joy is seen when the finished product is examined. A beautiful, delicate object fashioned out of skilful imagination. But just as models get broken and smashed, so the world, your creation, can be spoilt by man's violence and greed.

Lord, give us respect for what you have made.

OUR RESPONSE TO GOD'S GIFTS

O God, you have entrusted the resources of the world to our very human hands:
to tend the fields;
to use its harvests;
to conserve its riches.
As we consider our stewardship in our worship,
help us to be honest with ourselves and with you.

A DIALOGUE ON STEWARDSHIP

God and His Universe

The three parts may be taken by one of the leaders and two of the young people, or all by young people.

A. The Bible tells that in the beginning God made everything.

B. It also says that when he looked out upon it, he saw that it was very good.

C. There are still many lovely things within it – blue skies, white snow, sparkling clear water, majestic hills.

B. Don't forget the great forests and woods with the leaves of the trees so beautifully green in spring and so many-hued in autumn.

A. But if God made everything, why has so much of it turned nasty?

B. Like the forests cut down for timber and paper, and the sharp lines of the hills disfigured by slag heaps.

C. Yes, and the blue of the sky hidden behind the smog of our big cities; the whiteness of the snow churned into oozy slush in the streets; sparkling clear water stifled by pollutants.

A. It's still God's world.

B. But we built it our way.

C. And we rejected the Lord who gave us so many things to enjoy.

A. Lord, forgive us.

B. Help us to make a new start.

C. And help us to put right those things that can be put right.

HOW DO WE TREAT GOD'S WORLD?

We have a wonderful world, but how long will it last? We use up the resources of the earth at an alarming rate; the harvest of millions of years we burn up in the passing moments. The balance of nature, so carefully fashioned, is destroyed in our selfish quest for a comfortable life. The waste products of our affluent civilisation foul the rivers and make great lakes sterile. Birds and animals may find their breeding grounds a concrete waste, and species become extinct.

We read that 'God saw that it was good'. Help us, Lord, never to forget that it is your world we treat so selfishly.

THANKSGIVING FOR LOVELY THINGS

After each sentence the response is:
We thank you, God, for lovely things.

O God, we give you thanks for the lovely things in our cities and towns:
(R)

For fine buildings, good to look upon, whose graceful lines are a credit to the architect
(R)

For museums and art galleries, which house the treasures of past generations
(R)

For the mixture of ancient and modern, which helps us to sense the passage of time and yet of the eternity of God
(R)

For the open spaces, the parkland and the playing fields
(R)

For the gay colours in the gardens, brightly coloured doors, pretty curtains in the windows

(R)

For people, busy about their work, their chatter on the buses, their readiness to help the stranger

(R)

O God, help us to make our towns lovely places, where men and women and boys and girls can live worthwhile lives; through Jesus Christ our Lord.

A PRAYER FOR SCIENTISTS

After each sentence the response is:

Hear us, Lord, as we offer this prayer.

Lord, we pray for all scientists who try to ensure that man's exploitation of the wealth of the earth will not despoil the world you have made.

(R)

We pray for those who try to make safer the work of miners and fishermen.

(R)

We pray for those who try to find ways in which diseases like cancer may be overcome.

(R)

We pray for those who try to find new techniques for heart and kidney transplants.

(R)

We pray for all scientists that they may use their skills to enhance and enrich life.

(R)

THE NEEDS OF OTHERS

Lord, we recall the ancient law:

> 'When you reap the harvest in your land, you shall not reap right into the edges of your field, neither shall you glean the fallen ears. You shall leave them for the poor and for the alien.' *(Leviticus 23. 22, NEB)*

Lord, we have plenty to eat. Help us always to be grateful and not to forget the needs of others.

A REFLECTION ON HOLIDAYS

How lazy the river seemed as it meandered through the meadows; but how mighty the sea as it pounded the sea wall! What beauty as the crimson sun set across the vast reaches of the sea; how lovely to feel its warm rays as we sat on the beach! It was frightening looking at the crevasses as we climbed the hills; but what a reward as we looked out from the summit at the panorama about us!

No wonder, Lord, that the Bible says about the world you made: It was very good.

ELECTRICITY

The flashing light pierces the darkness across the waters and guides the ship safely into harbour. The electric fire brings its comforting warmth to the old couple huddled on the settee on a winter's night. The TV set brings the world to the old man who can never now leave his home. We take for granted the power of electricity that makes all this possible. And we forget that men take great risks to enable us to have it. The miners toil in the dark and the cold and the loneliness of the pit to harvest the coal that drives the turbines that produce the power that brings light and warmth, comfort and safety to so many.

Thank you, Lord, for them.

EXPLORERS

O Lord our God, we give thanks to you for all those great pioneers who have probed the mysteries and grandeur of the earth.

We thank you for explorers – people like Abraham who set off for the unknown never quite sure what they would find: those who have explored the polar regions; or discovered the sources of the great rivers; who have traversed the vast deserts of Africa; or probed the mysteries of the dense jungles of South America.

We thank you for the great travellers who have opened up for us highways across the seas; who braved the furies of the oceans; who sought the riches of the Orient; and admired the cultures of unknown civilisations.

We thank you, Lord, for the explorers of today; the astronauts who have reached across the vastness of space and probed the mysteries of the moon; who have opened to us the limitless possibilities of travel within the oceans of space; and have helped us to understand a little more clearly how wonderful is the world that you have made.

THE ANIMAL KINGDOM

Lord, we are told that before ever man inhabited the world, there were animals: fish, insects, reptiles and mammals. True, you made man in your own image as the crown of creation, but the world belongs to them as well as to us. We are ashamed at the way in which we abuse your creatures. We build motorways over their criss crossing tracks, and they are slaughtered by the machines we drive. Our cities encroach upon the fields and jungles which are their homes; we kill the lakes with our detergents; we poison the fields with our chemicals. Forgive us, Lord, that we have driven so many species from their natural home, and have imperilled them to the point of extinction.

True we love animals: cats and dogs and hamsters and

mice and rabbits. Give us, Lord, the same regard for all your creatures. We pray, Lord, for the organisations concerned with the care of animals.

Then Lord, there are the zoos. As children we enjoyed riding on the elephant. There is still fascination in watching the lion tear at his food or the seals gracefully catching the fish thrown to them for food. We are glad, Lord, to see some of the marvels in the animal kingdom that we would never see in their natural state. But help us, Lord, not to abuse animal life in our zoos.

Finally, we think of those most closely concerned with the preservation of threatened species. Lord, in our wild-life preserves and our nature preserves encourage those who seek to rescue species in danger of dying out.

REFLECTION ON THE SEASONS

Let us think of . . .

Spring
New life.
Lambs.
Washed green of the leaves.
Vivid yellow of the daffodils.
The glorious promise of summer.

Summer
The long, long days.
The seaside.
The vivid colours of the flowers.
Hot sun.
Long walks together.
Holidays.

Autumn
The quietness of the world of nature.
Falling leaves,
Browns and reds and yellows.

Winter
Snow and ice.
Bare trees.
Silent earth.
Dark and cold.
The long sleep of winter.

O God, who promised that while the earth remains, the seasons will not change, we thank you for the pattern of the seasons and the constancy of your love.

A MEDITATION FOR A RAINY DAY

It's raining, Lord.
It seems such a waste of a good day to be raining.
I've had to change my plans and now I'm stuck here
 brooding—or thinking—or praying?
Why does it have to rain?
Yes, Lord, the reservoirs were getting low.
And yes, Lord, I know that the crops need rain if we
 are to have a decent harvest.
But why does it have to rain when I had arranged to
 have a picnic with the group?
What's that you say, Lord?
A drought?
Where?
Oh, yes, I remember seeing the pictures on TV – cattle
 lying dead, children with bloated tummies.
I thought that pictures like that were only propaganda
 for Oxfam or Christian Aid or something.
Yes, Lord. I know now that it really happens.
But why does it always have to rain on me?
Lord, I'm selfish, I know.
Thank you for the rain that fills the reservoirs
 and waters the crops.
But let some of it fall in India or Africa or
 wherever there has been a drought.

3. Jesus Christ our Lord

A. *ADVENT AND CHRISTMAS*

PREPARING GOD'S WAY

Leader: What equipment have we, Lord, for preparing your way?

Everyone: We can work and play, laugh and cry;
we can think and plan, care and serve.

Leader: Is that enough, Lord, for preparing your way?

Everyone: . . . enough – in a cruel world?
. . . enough – with time running out?

Leader: And where shall we start, Lord, preparing your way?

Everyone: Here, Lord, here!

Two Voices: There are routes to be planned and roads to be built, from city to city, from person to person.

Everyone: Here, Lord, here!

Two Voices: There are people who are lost, with no roof overhead, with no faith in their hearts.

Everyone: Here, Lord, here!

Leader: Can we make a start here, Lord, preparing your way?

Everyone: Through our lives, Lord, PREPARE YOUR WAY.

THE FORERUNNER

O God, thank you for choosing a rebel like John the Baptist to prepare the way for your Son. May all who have his spirit learn to serve the same Lord, Jesus Christ.

THE LAST DAYS

Reader A: Imagine the last days!

Reader B: The last disc, the last kiss;
the last purchase, the last bell.
No more sound, no more argument;
still limbs, unmoving feet.
Time has run out.

Reader A: They could come, those last days,
unless we prepare a new way.

Reader B: Lord, help us to harness this planet's resources!
Help us to find peace on this planet!

Reader A: Imagine the last days!

Reader B: Jesus called them *festival days,*
the moment for a banquet,
the chance to dance and sing.
Jesus called them *God's days,*
days of fulfilment, days of grace.

Reader A: They could come, those last days,
if we prepare a new way.

Reader B: Lord, help us to listen to the news of God's grace!
Help us to follow his way!

A LOT OF PREPARATION TO DO

Holy Spirit, we've a lot of preparation to do:
Skills to master,
Arts to develop,
Experiences to learn from
in carrying responsibility,
in being responsible to others.

Some of this suits us; some of it does not. You are a welcome Friend, enlivening and encouraging. Because of your presence, we ask: May we not be dispirited, nor overwhelmed!

THE WORD MADE FLESH

Praised be the Word,
whose work was the foundation of all things.
Praised be the Spirit,
whose life gives life to all things.
Praised be the eternal Light,
never to be put out.
Praised be the Father's only Son,
the embodiment of Truth.

HAPPY CHRISTMAS

Lord God, it is surprisingly hard not to have a happy Christmas when so many people are trying to make it happy for us. Teach us the secret of enjoyment so that we ourselves spread joy and not gloom.

HOW GOD ACTED

There are many things, Lord, that I don't understand about Christmas. But one thing I can't escape. At Christmas you showed your usual way of getting things done – a human life. I should like to know a little more of what that means. Give me the patience and courage to find out.

IN BETHLEHEM!

We wonder, Lord, where Jesus has been born. Not on Mars, Jupiter, Neptune or Pluto, of that we're confident. In Bethlehem only, we suppose, in this vast galaxy – which is strange, considering the size of Bethlehem.

But outside this galaxy, where has Jesus been born? Or are there no other people in any other galaxy on an ark like earth? Why make us look for Jesus in this tiny planet in that tiny town? Your Old Testament people received special treatment – a mixed blessing they sometimes felt it: a lot to live for and a long way to fall! We earth-dwellers feel the same about our special treatment.

Could you make Christmas this time a moment to face up to the special privilege you have given us – that you could have chosen a million places – and you chose Bethlehem?

RESPONSE

Play a striking foreign celebration of the Nativity, like La Anunciación *from* 'Navidad Nuestra' *(Philips BL 7684).*

Leader: Let us pray:
For the joy of others which communicates itself to us . . .

All: *Thank you, Lord.*

Leader: For rhythm and melody, voice and lyric . . .

All: *Thank you, Lord.*

Leader: For the spectacular differences of national character . . .

All: *Thank you, Lord.*

Leader: For Jesus Christ, a joy to all men everywhere . . .

All: *Thank you, Lord.*

A HYMN OF REVOLUTION

It is God whom I praise.
It is my Deliverer for whom I sing.
For he showed great care to his servant,
and every generation will bless my fortune.
He can contrive anything – he has done so for me.
    'Holy', we call him.
    Worldwide is his grace, to everyone who fears him.
He has exercised power by the flourish of an arm.
He has put the high-minded to panic and flight.
He has dethroned rulers, given humble people prestige.
Hungry stomachs he gave a banquet of the best,
and the rich he despatched empty-handed.
He took the part of the ancient Israel,
so he never forgot his merciful promises
made to them, made to our ancestors –
to Abraham and his family –
to the end of time. *(Magnificat)*

THE CAVE

Lord, you gave man a cave to live in.
He found shelter there; it was his home.
He chiselled in its walls his hopes and fears.
He discovered there who he was,
that he could chip flint and sharpen stone,
and begin to order the world.

Lord, you gave your Son a cave.
In it the child of hope was born,
in it divine love came to birth.
In it was shown who man might be,
where man might find himself again.

They say, Lord, we may die in a cave,
a pre-stressed concrete grave,
victims of radiation and hate,
ending where we began.

Good Lord, our God, help us in imagination this Christmas to visit the cave of Bethlehem,
and learn there the secret of our humanity,
and the purpose for which we are here.

THREE GIFTS

What gifts today's wise men bring to him!

First:
the shining metals of technology;
the researched wisdom of ancient cities;
the passionate justice of the East.
Second:
the cathedrals of stone and sound;
the offerings of the human spirit;
the ancient responses to God's call.
Third:
the anguish of human progress;
the continuing struggle of evolving man;
the martyrdom of human freedom.

Our gold, our frankincense, our myrrh.

And why do the wise men bring them?

Do they arrive proud of their achievements, their enterprise and their courage?
Or have they discovered – from someone, somewhere – that these are part of our homage to the Only Wise?
And can they understand the value they possess at the feet of Jesus Christ, the Great Renewer?

Leader: Here is URANIUM – refined from ore – a sign of power – rods for reactors.
Is this an offering for the Christ?

All: The world is yours. Receive our gift. May it be used for life and health.

Leader: Here is PAINTING – a product of time and expense – a sign of dedication – a flash-point of discipline and freedom.
Is this an offering for the Christ?

All: The world is yours. Accept our gift. May it serve your purpose well.

Leader: Here is MEDICINE – researched and tested – subsidised and prescribed – mitigating man's pain.
Is this an offering for the Christ?

All: The world is yours. Accept our gift. May it be properly used.

Leader: The wise men bring their gifts, Lord.

All: Lord, renew your world.

B. *LENT*

PREPARATION

Lord, may we use this time before Easter so effectively in preparation of mind, body and spirit that, when Easter comes, we may really catch its spirit.

TESTING

Tests, tests, tests. We are for ever being tested, Lord. The tests you had to suffer – did you always know why? Scripture says: 'Tested, every way, as we are, without sin.' You can help us, during this period of testing, to grow and not to recede.

PREPARING FOR LIFE

Lord Jesus, you made vital decisions about the kind of life you intended to live. Thank you for your example. In moments like these may we discover the strength to follow suit. May your Spirit, which led you into the wilderness, accompany us too.

THE WILDERNESS

The wilderness has its appeal, Lord.
A hermit has few worries.
No fear there of being hurt.
No timetable to keep to.
Solitariness, peace, simplicity.
I could go for that life.

But there seemed little peace
 when you entered the wilderness, Lord.
You found there an iron resolve
 that not even the shadow of the Cross could shake.
You found there strict priorities
 so that your powers would not dissipate themselves.
You found an overriding sense of God's sovereignty.
I don't find that kind of life so easy to go for.

I need to know where I should go, Lord.
There is an attraction about peace, solitariness, simplicity.
Your way is compelling, Lord. But different – and hard.

May the Sovereign Father, the Crucified Son,
 and the Energising Spirit, one God for ever, see me on the right road.

DREAM AND REALITY

Lord God, we often dream of the future. You encourage us in planning and believing. We are grateful that you made us forward-looking. We are grateful for man, the imaginative creation. Sometimes our dreams are given a sudden change of direction – a letter, a friendship, an interview. We are grateful that we can be excited about the future. We are grateful for life, with its unfathomable interest.

But some days are dull and boring, Lord. The ordinary takes over. Interest dwindles. Forgive us if we resent this. Forgive us too, Lord, if we forget the dream, and live each day for itself, for the kicks we can get from it.

We pray for your help. Help us to avoid what might wreck our dreams finally. Help us on the hard days to keep our anticipation alive. Help us to swallow the hard reality that belongs with the dream.

CONSERVATION

Lord God, we are concerned about your world. The world must use its resources properly, otherwise there will be so much extravagance, so much waste.

And, Lord God, make us match this concern in our personal lives. Show us how to use our resources properly, resources of energy, pocket, intellect. Don't let us condemn others for an extravagance we allow ourselves. We don't want to be hypocrites, Lord. But it is difficult to achieve in our own lives the standards we can see are right for others. Give us the courage of consistency; we ask this, Lord, in your power.

FREEDOM

O Lord God,
freedom is great to watch!
A sparrow freed from an attic,
a kestrel swooping by the motorway,
the punching style of an athlete,
the flowing line of a team attack,
a cellist's sweeping bow.
Freedom is great to watch!
A novelist daring to print the unpleasant truth,
a nation earning the right to self-government.

But, Lord, it worries me that freedom costs so much – all the dedication, care and skill, if freedom is not to be just a vicious form of slavery.

You have made me free, Lord, gloriously free. Sometimes I sense the cost of my freedom, and the vicious slavery into which I might so easily slip. The inner habits and passions, the outer, destructive ideas pose a threat which you, Lord, must help me to understand, in your grace.

C. *JESUS CHRIST, THE WAY, THE TRUTH, AND THE LIFE*

ACT OF THANKSGIVING

Leader: For showing us true love,
All: **Jesus Christ, we thank you.**

Leader: For showing us true life,
All: **Jesus Christ, we thank you.**

Leader: Our life, our truth, our way,
All: **Jesus Christ, we thank you.**

JESUS AT THE BEGINNING

You began everything, Lord,
  everything that exists.

You began everything, Lord,
  everything we now enjoy.

You began everything, Lord,
  before man began.

You began everything, Lord,
  and you yourself were born!

JESUS THE SERVANT

Lord Jesus, you did not treat divinity as if it consisted in receiving – prayers, vows, gifts, homage, worship – but only in giving – sacrificially, humbly, lovingly. Therefore yours is the name above every name. *Alleluia!*

JESUS' POWER

Lord Jesus Christ, we see your earthly power and the economy with which you used it. May all men, whatever authority they hold, see the sense of your example. For you live and reign with God: Father, Son and Holy Spirit.

THE APRON

A leather apron,
a bowl of cold water,
a towel . . .
  pairs of stained, tired feet . . .

You came, Lord Jesus, meeting simple needs with uncommon devotion: 'As I have loved you, you are to love one another,' you said.

Let us in silence think of any simple needs of our neighbours which we could meet. *(Pause)*

At moments when there are worthwhile jobs to be done may we be ready to act.

JESUS, YESTERDAY, TODAY AND FOR EVER

Who were you, Lord?
A joker, a jester, a brigand, a zealot,
a rabbi, a teacher, a wonderful healer?

Who were you, Lord?
Does the answer depend on the person I ask?

Who were you, Lord?
You won a name that your movement never lost.
You spoke repeatedly in the authority of God.
You survived the worst that your enemies could do.

Who were you, Lord?
'I am the same,' he replies, 'yesterday, today and for ever.'

May we know you, the same yesterday, today and for ever, and set this knowledge alongside all our attempts to understand the meaning of your earthly work.

ACCEPTANCE IN THE KINGDOM

There is no one outside your kingdom, Lord. So may we make no one feel unwanted, but reflect in our attitudes the breadth of your kingdom's scope. The leper expected rejection. The Samaritan expected the cold shoulder. What the tax-collector found – they all found – acceptance, at the coming of the kingdom.

Show us, Lord, in all we learn or experience, the quality of divine love which seeks us out, accepts us, and reclaims us.

POPULARITY

Save us, Lord, from the shallowness of conviction that always shouts with the demonstrators.

(Fade in part of a Top Ten disc)

Let us pray for people enjoying popularity. Give them,

Lord, a sane view of themselves, so that if the tide turns against them they may ride disfavour without becoming cynical and warped.

DOING JESUS' WORK

Lord, make me a helper.
Let the words on my lips today be as your words to someone in need.
Let my hands be as your hands reaching out to someone lonely.
Let my feet take me on your errands of mercy.

THE VICTORY OF THE CROSS

Your Cross, Lord, gathers to itself all the suffering we have seen and read of. It is the sign of your victory over the world. It is the sign of your wonderful love for the world.

O God, you sent your Son. He died on the Cross. We praise you for the victory of his Cross.

KEEP FAITH

Judas betrayed his friend. He thought he had every excuse. But he broke faith and suffered the consequences.

Lord, save us from the name of 'traitor' whatever may tempt us and whatever excuses are to hand. May we never break faith with you.

VICTORY IN DEFEAT

I know, Lord, what defeat is like.

I have seen it a thousand times.
It is failing to do what I know I ought to do.
It is the agony of seeing a runner
overtake me at the tape.
It is the unsuccessful effort to keep a trust
I didn't deserve.

Lord, I know defeat when I see it.

Your Cross can never be called defeat – or else it is a stranger kind than I have ever met. For through it you have won your way into the hearts of men everywhere. Therefore we sing your praises, crucified Lord, victim and victor.

RISEN!

Risen Lord, your resurrection is like a clear and lovely dawn after a night of worry and uncertainty. We can get up and live again.

Christ is risen. Alleluia!

OUR LIVING LORD

Christ, joining our human conversation,
  illuminating our common study,
Christ, entering our home as an unknown guest,
Christ of the Emmaus Road,
  be a living Lord for us.

AFFIRMATION

Why go on?
Why befriend the lonely?
Why restore the desperate?
Why struggle to be understanding?
Why go on hoping for an easing of tension?

I could not give an answer, Lord. An honest answer would be hard to find. It would seem far easier to give up, to call it an unequal struggle and have done with it.

The answer I could not give you have given. Your rising affirms this way of life as right, the way of care and restoration. You are a living affirmation of the way of love. For this answer to our question, we are thankful, Lord.

4. The Holy Spirit

SPIRIT OF POWER

We thank you, Lord God, for Pentecost, for the coming of your Spirit's power that inspired the first disciples to become brave and adventurous preachers and missionaries, and filled the Church with faith and joy and love.

May that same presence and power uplift and inspire our lives, so that we may be transformed into the kind of people you want us to be.

SPIRIT OF LIFE AND LIGHT AND LOVE

Spirit of life,
  inspire our lives with yours.
Spirit of light,
  shine through all we do.
Spirit of love,
  give us loving hearts.

A MEDITATION ON THE SPIRIT

I stood at the window the other day,
and I saw the shape of the wind.
I watched it blowing through the grass in the field,
in long swirling sweeps, and short gusts.
Each time it blew, the field moved and swayed at its touch.
I couldn't see where the wind came from, nor where it went, but I saw its shape in the grass.

The Spirit of God is like wind –
he blows where he wills;
you don't know where he comes from, nor where he is going, but he leaves his mark.
Lord, make me sensitive to your Spirit's presence,
that my life may be shaped by him.

THE SPIRIT AT WORK IN US

Holy Spirit, you are always at work in us, teaching us to live by what is true and good. Yet so often we ignore you, and reject what you try to teach us. Forgive us for those times

when we have known the right and chosen
the wrong,
when we have known the truth and told a lie,
when we have made a promise and not kept it,
when we should have stayed calm but lost our
self-control,
when we have seen someone needing help and done
nothing about it,
when we have seen your will for us, but thought we
knew better.

Holy Spirit, make us more ready to respond to you,
so that we grow into the people you mean us to be.

JOY IN LIVING

A prayer written by a teenager.

Spirit of God,
as we go through this world,
working and playing,
caring only for ourselves,
guide us toward your love,
give us joy in living.
Too often we are selfish,
not bothering about those in need.
Help us to help them,
that they too may have joy in living.

A DIALOGUE: LOVE, THE SPIRIT'S GREATEST GIFT

First Reader: 'All you need is love.'
That's what the pop-song said.

Second Reader: But what *is* true love?

First Reader: That's difficult to put into words.
The best way to understand love is to see it at work.
Love, for example, is visiting an old lady who is lonely.

Second Reader: Love is making friends with someone nobody else wants.

First Reader: Love is taking the first step to make up a quarrel.

Second Reader: Love is helping a person in need without expecting any credit or pat on the back.

First Reader: Love is doing someone a favour even if it costs you something.

Second Reader: Love is standing up for what you believe in in the face of opposition.

First Reader: Love is forgiving your enemies.

Second Reader: Love is dying on a cross for the sake of others.

First Reader: Holy Spirit, we thank you
for your greatest gift of all –
the gift of love.

THE HARVEST OF THE SPIRIT

(Based on Galatians 5.22, 23)

O Holy Spirit, produce in us those qualities which are the harvest of your presence.

Spirit of God, fill us with love –
    not love of self,
    but a selfless concern to serve you and others.
(Pause)

Spirit of God, give us joy –
    the sheer delight of knowing that your love for us is greater than we can ever imagine. *(Pause)*

Spirit of God, grant us peace –
    that quiet sense of security that is based on the certainty of your presence. *(Pause)*

Spirit of God, give us meekness –
    the gentleness which is also strong. *(Pause)*

Spirit of God, teach us self-control –
    the ability to be in charge of ourselves, that our words and deeds may glorify you. *(Pause)*

We ask this prayer in the name of him in whom the harvest of the Spirit was most perfectly seen, Jesus our Lord.

FAITH, HOPE, LOVE

Holy Spirit, giver of all good gifts,
we ask you to grant us
    a deeper faith,
    a stronger hope,
    a greater love.

THE SPIRIT GIVES LIFE

Spirit of life,
we pray for all for whom life seems empty:
for the person who finds no joy or challenge in life;
for the man who gets no satisfaction from his work;
for the old lady who recently lost her husband;
for the youth who is hooked on drugs;
for the family without a home or regular income;
for the man who craves alcohol;
for all who do not care about Jesus Christ.

Spirit of life,
to such people, and to all who help them,
bring new hope and new purpose.
Show them how to find their way
from death to life.

GIFTS OF THE SPIRIT

All the different talents men have, Lord God, are the gifts of your Spirit. Whether they are gifts of mind, body or spirit, they come from him.

We thank you for the things we are good at, for the talents we have.

Help us not to be jealous of those whose gifts seem greater than ours, not to feel resentful about people who get more of the limelight.

Teach us to be glad for their sake, and to use to the full what we have.

THE SPIRIT'S INFLUENCE

The response is: **We give you our praise and thanks.**

For your presence in the Church and in the world, for your influence in every part of men's lives,
Spirit of the living God . . .

For the insight you give to scientists and technologists, for the care and skill of doctors and nurses,
Spirit of the living God . . .

For the way you inspire musicians and painters, thinkers, writers, poets, actors,
Spirit of the living God . . .

For challenging us to serve other people, helping us to give of our time and energy,
Spirit of the living God . . .

For your presence and power in the lives of Christians, enabling them to become more and more Christlike,
Spirit of the living God . . .

THANKSGIVING TO FATHER, SON AND HOLY SPIRIT

The leader could read the words at each point, the young people repeating them after him.

Father, you made the world and all that it contains;
you created us in your own image, able to communicate with you;
you care for us, and you have proved your love for us by the gift of Jesus our Lord.
To you, eternal Father: **We offer our humble thanks.**

Lord Jesus Christ, you gave your life for mankind;
you have given us the opportunity to be re-created, to be reconciled to God.
Your living presence is always with us.
To you, eternal Son: **We offer our humble thanks.**

Holy Spirit, you are at work in the life of the world, sustaining, inspiring, renewing;
you can create in us afresh the image of God, and help us to become more and more like Jesus.
Your power can change our lives.
To you, eternal Spirit: **We offer our humble thanks.**

A DIALOGUE ON THE TRINITY

First Reader: If we are really honest, we have to admit that we find the idea of the Trinity difficult.

Second Reader: 'One in three and three in one' –
the Church has believed and taught it
for a very long time;
but what does it really mean?

First Reader: Even if we can't understand it completely it may help if we use an illustration.

Think of the sea stretching before us,
and someone at the water's edge.
How does he know the sea is there?

Second Reader: In a number of ways:
he can see it and hear it;
he can smell it, touch and even taste it.

First Reader: So he experiences the sea in different ways. But it is always the same sea.

And Christians experience God in different ways – for them he is a loving Father, he is Jesus the Son,
he is the power of the Holy Spirit.
But it is always the same God.

Both Readers: For the greatness and the mystery of your being, Lord God, we worship you. But you are also our Friend, and for that we praise you too.

5. Our Response

A. *PENITENCE*

BEING SORRY FOR THE PAST

(a)

There are some things in our lives, Lord, that we ought to turn our back on. Lapses of memory that have hurt our friends, vicious acts in a moment of temper. We ask for strength to face up to them, and put them right where we can. Where we cannot, help us to understand the consequences of what we have done and to commit them to you.

You have promised forgiveness to those who look to you in sincerity for a new beginning. We go now, confident in your love.

(b)

For wasting our time,
for neglecting our prayers,
for refusing to listen to good advice,
for turning a deaf ear to someone in need,
for taking our own way without consulting you,
Good Lord, forgive us.

B. *DISCIPLESHIP*

BELONGING

We belong to the family of God,
  a family without limits.
We belong to the family of God,
  where all grow up into Christ.
We belong to the family of God,
  praising you with one voice,
  and praying: 'Our Father . . . '

Where are the trumpets, Lord?
  Trumpets to sound to your glory.
  Trumpets to wake your people.
  Trumpets to announce to the world:
    He is King!
    He is Lord!
    God is sovereign for ever!

POSITIVE PRAYER

I want to live a positive life, Lord Jesus, living with zest for the world and for you. May my prayers help me to do that. May they gather up all my determination, all my zest, and interpret the way I live.

And may they find a response from you, Lord Jesus, for you are God's positive stamp on all creation.

PRAYER AND LIFE

Holy Spirit, unfold the tiny moments of our prayer until they cover the whole course of our lives with your blessing.

C. *COMMITMENT*

LOOKING TO JESUS

Your disciples said: 'To whom shall we go? You have the words of eternal life.' We respond, Lord, as they did and look for your direction.

OPEN MINDS

Give us open minds and hearts, Lord, open to others in school and club, so that we listen and try to understand. Give us also a firm faith, firm in commitment to you and in knowledge of you, so that our lives are not spent at the mercy of everyone's opinion.

SEARCH FOR TRUTH

Teach us, Lord Christ, to search for the truth wherever we are and whatever we are doing, without fear of what we might discover. Prepare us also for the discovery that we are as likely to be overtaken by truth as to overtake it ourselves.

CALLED TO SERVE

Your call to serve, Lord, is a challenge.
It isn't always easy. Sometimes we fail.
But nothing is more worthwhile.
Help us to put our whole selves into it,
and help us to know that
when you give us a task to do,
you give us the strength to do it.

D. *PERSONAL GROWTH*

'*. . . so shall we fully grow up into Christ.*'

(Ephesians 4. 15, NEB)

GROWTH

(a)

O God, we offer to you the rich experience of growing. New life, liberating, frustrating, exuberant, belongs to you, just as it comes from you.

(b)

Our growth enables us to see in greater range the height and breadth and length of your love, O Lord our God.

We are all children of your love, and you have called us to serve you together. For the experience of growth we thank you, Lord.

FITTING IN

If I'm tempted to ask, Lord,
'Why did he have to come here?' or
'How can I be myself with him around?'
help me to see reason.
Perhaps it's just that you have
a strong sense of humour –
or just that I haven't.

GROWING OUT OF THINGS

Sometimes my ideas are like my shoes, Lord. They pinch when I grow out of them! Help me find some new ones that fit!

WHEN I NEED SPECIAL HELP

So many came to you, Lord Jesus, asking for help.
Some were ill.
Some were sad.
Some were well.
Some were bad.
None of them went away disappointed.
Lord, help me.

RELYING ON GOD

Jeremiah said, and Moses said – 'Try someone older, Lord'. We would try to serve you as we are, perhaps learn from our mistakes, but trust you to know what we can do.

LIVING WHILE OTHERS WATCH

With others looking on, Lord God, often our concentration slips and our standard of performance drops. May that not happen, Lord, as we try to follow your way. Help us to find the maturity to live, while others watch, in the way that you require of us, day by day.

All of us at times have problems, Lord. There may be a problem at home, at school, or at work. We may be going through a difficult time with a friend, or perhaps have a difficult decision to make. Maybe we have trouble controlling our temper, or overcoming some temptation. Maybe we have doubts about our faith.

Help us to remember that Jesus himself experienced difficult times. He knew agonising moments of decision and choice. He knew what it was to be let down. He knew suffering and pain.

May we never run away from problems, Lord. Like Jesus, may we face them with courage. And may we never forget, whatever problems we face, that you are with us.

E. *MORAL CHOICES*

THE VOICE OF CONSCIENCE

Yours are the prophets calling for reform.
  Lord God, alert our conscience, we pray.

A WARNING

Before we throw away the guide-lines which others have left us, help us to be sure what we are doing.

MONEY

'What is this cash worth, Lord?'
    A boutique fashion to perk up my spirits?
    or a birthday cassette for a friend?
    or to put away for a rainy day?
    or a packet or so of fags? . . .
    or a contribution to Oxfam
    or to the Church's stewardship scheme? . . .
Lord, help me to re-phrase the question:
'What is *all* my cash worth, Lord?'
But there you don't give me a direct answer.
So help me to work at it, Lord –
until I find the answer that's right – for me.

A PRAYER FOR INTEGRITY

(Suitable after talks on sex, drugs, etc.)

We've listened Lord.
We're the people who have to decide.
Experience and expert opinion – that's one thing.
Our responsibility is another.
At least, Lord, may the
integrity of those who advised us
be reflected in how we behave,
for the sake of Jesus Christ.

SPITE

Lord, if I ever do things to spite people, forgive me for being so irrational.

CIVIL DISOBEDIENCE

What ought we to be building, Lord? How ought we to build? Can the illegal ever be a foundation on which to build for the future? And are the examples of others – well-established acts of disobedience – fair parallels to what we do? All these and many other questions, Lord, help us to sort out, now.

COMPROMISE

Lord, I must stand on my own feet, independent in judgement, master of my own mind.

Lord, I must learn to live with my family and my friends, although they may not think as I do.

Supply me with courage to believe that I could be right, and with humility to know that I could be wrong.

6. The Church

THE CHURCH IS PEOPLE

What's the first thing we think of when we hear the word 'Church'? A building, the pulpit, a stained-glass window? But more important than building and furnishings are the people. They are the Church.

So now we give thanks, Father, for your people everywhere, bound together by their worship and by the ties of Christian love.

Thank you, Father, for the example of Christians who have died; keep us faithful to the gospel they believed in. *(Pause)*

Thank you for the life of the Church overseas and for the witness of Christians who are suffering for their faith. *(Pause)*

Thank you for the movement, here and abroad, towards further church unity, and for ways in which churches are working together. *(Pause)*

Thank you for all the Christians of this neighbourhood, for their witness and their work in our community. *(Pause)*

Thank you for the part that we ourselves can play in your Church that stretches down the years and across the world.

THE ROCK ON WHICH THE CHURCH IS BUILT

The truth about Peter
is that he was not outstandingly religious or holy,
but an ordinary human being.
He was sometimes sensible, sometimes thoughtless;
he could be courageous, he could be cowardly.
He was impulsive, outspoken, and not very reliable.

And yet, Lord Jesus, you chose him;
unreliable as he was, you called him the 'Rock',
and were prepared to build your Church on him –
on him, and people like him.

Thank you, Lord, for calling people like ourselves,
and for being prepared to rely on us.
Just as Peter gradually became the rock you called him
to be,
make us rocklike and faithful to you.

THE GIFT OF THE CHURCH

A prayer written by a teenager.

Lord God, thank you for bringing your Church to this
world.
May its joy be shared everywhere and by everyone,
so that all may respect you as King of all the earth.

CHURCHGOING

Why do we come to church? It's a good question. Maybe out of habit, or a sense of duty. Maybe because it's a good place to meet our friends. Maybe we find it helpful. Whatever our reason, Lord, help us in our worship to reach out beyond ourselves, to catch a glimpse of your glory and goodness, and to offer ourselves to you in faith and love.

WORSHIP

If each of us was asked to list our chief interests, the list would probably be different in each case. All sorts of things would be included: sport, television, reading, food, hobbies, pop-stars, clothes, music . . .

Different people choose different things, but one thing is sure – whatever our chief interests may be, they are very important to us, and we are prepared to spend a lot of time on them. Sometimes they may mean so much to us that it could almost be said that we worship them.

Lord, may you be so much more important to us than any of these things, that we shall be prepared to give our time to worshipping you, and serving you in our lives.

WATER, BREAD AND WINE

A badge on a coat,
a ring on a finger,
a flag flying in the breeze –
all are symbols with a meaning,
each one stands for something important.

We thank you, Lord, for the symbols used
in the sacraments of the Church:
for the symbol of water in Baptism
to remind us that your love can make us clean;
for the symbols of bread and wine in Communion
to remind us that Jesus' life was given for us.

We thank you, Lord, for the way in which these ordinary things of life teach us eternal truths.

IN CHRIST'S COMMUNITY

Father, we thank you for things we belong to:
clubs, societies, school, our own group of friends.
We enjoy the company of other people,
and the things we have in common.

Help us, Father, to feel that we belong
to the family of your Church.
Teach us that within your Church
people of all kinds and all ages can be united
in their worship of you
and their service of others.

THE BODY OF CHRIST

It may seem strange to call the Church 'the body of Christ',
but that is what it is.
We thank you, our Father, for the challenge to be
Christ's body in the world today,
continuing what he began so long ago.
Help us then, as a body, and as individuals,
to offer as he did the good news of your love,
to care as he did for people who are in need,
to live our lives as he did to the glory of your name.

JAMIE

We think today of a man named Jamie.
He's a man in his forties, though he looks very much older.
Jamie is an alcoholic.
He neglects himself, drinks meths, dosses down where he can.
People call him a down-and-out.
Jamie stands for all the alcoholics and addicts,
all the helpless, lonely drop-outs, all the unwanted of our society.

As we think of this man today, Lord,
we ask you to remind us again of the Church's calling
to help the afflicted,
to go to the unwanted,
to care for the forgotten.
May the whole Church, and we ourselves, do all in our power to carry on what Christ began,
to love and help, as Jesus did, the Jamies of this world.

OUR OWN CHURCH

After each sentence the response is:
Father, hear our prayer.

We pray for our church, and all who come here,
that the Spirit of Jesus may be found in all we do.
Father, hear our prayer.

We ask you to bless our services,
that through our worship we may draw closer to you.
Father, hear our prayer.

We pray for all the activities of our church,
that young and old alike may grow in the Christian life.
Father, hear our prayer.

We ask your Spirit to guide the leaders of this church,
that they may carry out their responsibilities faithfully and well.
Father, hear our prayer.

We ask you to save our church from being too wrapped up in itself,
and to make us effective in our locality by our example and service.
Father, hear our prayer.

We ask you to give us all a real community spirit
as we serve the same Lord and care for one another.
Father, hear our prayer.

NOBODY IS PERFECT

'Nobody is perfect!' How true that saying is of the Church! But the Church doesn't claim to be a society for the perfect, but a company of imperfect people trying to become what God wants them to be.

O God, our lives are such a mixture –
we can be generous, we can be selfish,
in charge of ourselves, out of control,
kind and considerate, thoughtless and spiteful.

Yes – we confess, Lord, that the Church is imperfect, and we confess our own share in that, our own failure to live as we should.

But we thank you, Lord, for the knowledge that you accept us just as we are, with all our failures, and that you encourage us to strive to become like Jesus. He is our goal.

Help us, and your whole Church, to press on towards it.

7. The Bible

GOD SPEAKS THROUGH THE WORD

(a)

We use words to communicate,
face to face,
over long distances by telephone,
even between earth and moon.
Thank you, Lord, for the gift of words,
and for your message communicated to us
through the words of the Bible.

(b)

Grant, Father, that as we read the Bible your Holy Spirit will bring understanding to our minds and new meaning to our lives.

(c)

We can read the news in the daily paper, Lord, then leave it on one side. When we read the news of your love in the Bible, it can change our lives.

PRAYER FOR BIBLE SUNDAY

O God, we thank you for the gift of the Bible. We thank you for the Bible's story of your dealings with men, and for their living experiences recorded there. Above all, we thank you for all that we learn in its pages of your power and love, which we see supremely in Jesus Christ.

Help us to read the Bible regularly and with faith and humility, so that it brings us closer to you, and enriches our daily lives.

BOOKS – AND THE BIBLE

Lord, we should be lost without books –
books with interest and excitement,
books that make us laugh,
books that are more serious,
books that teach us about the world and about life.
Thank you, Lord, for books of all kinds.
Thank you especially for the Bible and the truths it contains.

THANKS FOR THE BIBLE

After each sentence, the response is:
We praise your name, O Lord.

For the writers and compilers of the Bible,
and their inspired understanding of your ways:
We praise your name, O Lord.

For the Bible's variety and colour,
for its history, poetry, legends, parables:
We praise your name, O Lord.

For those scholars and translators
through whose dedicated work men can read the Bible today:
We praise your name, O Lord.

For the devoted work of individuals, and Bible Societies,
in distributing Bibles throughout the world:
We praise your name, O Lord.

Teach us, O Lord, to value the Bible not only because it tells us of you, but also because it has meant so much to people over the centuries. May it mean as much to us.

THE BIBLE AND OURSELVES

May we never forget that the Bible is about real people – human beings very much like ourselves, who felt and behaved as we do: who could be sad and depressed, happy and cheerful, bad-tempered and selfish, kind and thoughtful – just like us.

The Bible describes so many human experiences –
David and Jonathan knew the real meaning of friendship and loyalty;
Amos was fierce and angry in demanding obedience to God;
Peter wept when he knew he had denied his Lord;
Martha was cross because she had to do all the housework;
Judas was weak enough to betray Jesus to the authorities;
Paul was brave enough to suffer hardship and imprisonment for his faith.

Help us, Father, to think of the Bible as a living book: telling us so much about real people, so much about ourselves, and so much about God's concern for us all.

ABOUT THE BIBLE

A prayer by a teenager.

Father God, day after day we see your book, the story of your love, gathering dust on a shelf. Perhaps we might take it down and read the stories of Joseph, Moses or Jonah.

Help us to see that there is more to the Bible than 'adventure' stories. Give us the power to read and understand all of your holy word.

A CONFESSION

Father, forgive us:

The Bible has so many important things to tell us, but we are often so unwilling to listen.

It speaks of all that God has done for us,
but we show so little love and thanks in return.

It tells us how people should treat each other,
but our pride and self-interest often take the place of love.

It describes how Jesus courageously obeyed God to the end, while we sometimes haven't the courage even to begin to do his will.

Father, forgive us. Help us to be more ready to listen to the truths of the Bible, and to act upon them.

WHO AM I?

Who am I, Lord?
To some people I'm just a name on a list,
to others just a number.
I get the feeling that I hardly matter.
Our planet is only a tiny speck in a vast universe,
and of the millions of people on this earth
I am only one.
Who am I, Lord? How can I matter?

But in the Bible we read
the good news that everybody counts.
Including me.
I'm not just a number stored in a computer;
I'm not just a name on a list.
I'm a person.
I'm me.
I matter, Lord, because I matter to you.
Every single person is precious in your sight.

Who am I, Lord?
I am a human being, and proud of it;
for if I matter to you,
then I really am someone.

8. Life at Home

LORD OF THE HOME

Lord of the home, we adore you; you have so made us that we find life best fulfilled in the life of the family. Make your treasures known to us amid the sacredness of family life.

OUR FATHER

'Our Father, who art in heaven . . .' Jesus taught us to pray these words. Father, you hallow all family life. You are there in the happiness of the family; there, too, in its problems and strife. May we never forget that you are 'Our Father'.

A PRAYER FOR FORGIVENESS

The response is: **Father, we really are sorry.**

It seems sometimes that those we love best of all, we try to hurt the most

(R)

For the bouts of temper, when we said things that hurt

(R)

For always demanding and not realising how much we were demanding

(R)

For not even noticing how tired other people were while we sat down and let them work

(R)

For our thoughtlessness and intolerance and disobedience, and sometimes for just being deliberately awkward and unpleasant

(R)

Help us, our Father, to be what in our better moments we want to be.

PARENTS

(a)

Lord, parents are such a problem! They do so much for us; they demand so much from us.

Thank you, Lord, for our parents:
Just for their being there;
For making home what it is;
For providing us with the thousand and one things we take for granted.

Help them Lord, to be patient with me.
I know I can be secretive and morose when they want to talk to me.
I know I play my record-player louder than their ears can stand.
I know I can be stubborn and rebellious.

Help me, Lord to be patient with my parents.
They have their reasons when they want me home earlier than I think they ought.
There are rules to be kept if the house is to run smoothly.

May I remember above all, Lord, what I am sure is true, that they really love me even when I am mad with them, and when they appear to be mad with me.

(b)

'Parents are a dead loss.' I've said that often enough. And then I remember my dinner . . . my dirty shirt . . . my torn jeans . . . And I recall how patient Dad is when I go fishing and what fun he is at the football match . . . Thank you, God, for Mum and Dad!

GRANDPARENTS

Gran (Grandad) is so funny! . . . She loves to talk about a world I do not know and of days long ago. Yet she has a wisdom that doesn't age. Her practical common sense is a great help to me. Help me to do what I can to make her days easy.

HOBBIES AND RELAXATION

Thank you, Lord, that when I get home from school, and have done my share of chores at home, and finished my homework, I can relax.

My stamp album is my way to explore the exciting countries of the world.

I can create something attractive out of a length of cotton material.

The pictures I see in my mind's eye I can transfer on to canvas or paper.

Thank you, Lord, too, for the open air; the football pitch and the tennis court; the woods and the hills to explore.

But thank you, too, that I don't have to be selfish with my leisure. There is fun, as well as drudgery in running errands, and digging Mr. Smith's garden. Thank you, Lord, anyway, for the good feeling I have when I have helped someone to do something they could not have done themselves.

A MEDITATION ON HOMEWORK AND HOUSEWORK

They tell me that I will know the difference when I have to go out to work! It seems to me there is plenty of work to do now! And I have to go to school as well! My satchel is always full of books when I go home. The maths problems don't work out. The history is boring. But if I switch on the television I get shouted at:

Have you finished your homework?
Then what about cleaning your shoes ready for the morning?
You haven't done the wiping up yet.
Are you going to take the dog for his walk?
Don't forget to tidy your bedroom.

Work? Life is all work – do this – do that. But, Lord, thank you that I am able to work. Thank you for those who care enough about me that they mark my homework carefully.

Thank you that I have a real place in the life of my home with jobs to do like the rest of the family. Thank you that we belong together and that life at home is good.

A VIEW FROM THE KITCHEN WINDOW

Jesus spoke about the lilies of the field and of the fields being ready for harvest. I am sure he must have been able to see those flowers from the house where he lived. All I can see is row upon row of houses; mill chimneys; pavements glistening in the rain. Old Mrs. Jones shambling down the road to the shops. The post box on the corner. Telegraph poles and lamp-posts. A town – busy and dirty; yet throbbing with life. Men and women; boys and girls; people – some I know, and some I don't.

Sometimes I think I would love to have a garden to look at instead. Maybe a lawn, green and flat – big enough to play cricket on. And flowers – big bright flowers. And an apple tree. And vegetables, of course, peas and beans and potatoes.

Yet this is my home. Thank you, Lord, for all the busy world that passes by outside my window.

WHEN HOME IS NOT HOME

A Dialogue Prayer.

A. I'm always glad to get back home.

B. It's all right for us; we know that Mum or Dad will always be there. What if you had to go into an empty house after school?

A. And get my own tea?

B. If you can find any tea to get!

A. My mum likes to have everything tidy. It gets tedious sometimes – put those handkerchiefs in the drawer – go and make your bed tidy.

B. But at least then you know where everything is; and it is more comfortable to go to bed when the bed is tidy! If your mum didn't care how things looked, you would be the first to grumble.

A. That's true. I know I grumble when Dad gets at me because I am a few minutes late getting in at night. But at least he cares enough to know what time I get in.

B. It must be awful when parents don't bother about you and let you do what you like, when you like.

A. Yes, and think of all the times we have grumbled about the rules we are expected to keep at home.

B. How much pocket money do you get?

A. Not as much as I would like!

B. But enough to do some of the things you like to do?

A. Oh yes. Not like one of my mates at school who is always scrounging. He doesn't get pocket money. No wonder some youngsters resort to stealing.

B. It's funny isn't it? You think of home as the house you live in.

A. But it's more than that. It's the people who live there, and the way they care for each other.

B. Thank God for a home where you can be yourself.

A. And be loved.

B. Where home is home.

BROKEN HOMES

Lord Jesus, you know what living in a family is all about. You know what it is like too when the family is broken; you had to become the breadwinner after Joseph had died. Lord, we pray for families where mother or father has died. We pray for families that are divided or broken because mother or father has left home. We pray for families where there is stress and tension. Lord, may they find in you the help and security they need.

9. Life with Other People

THANKS FOR THOSE WHO SERVE US

The response is: **Thanks be to God.**

For all who help to make life so satisfying.

(R)

For the people upon whom we depend to provide us with food, electricity, gas and water.

(R)

For those whose skills make possible the TV programmes we enjoy, the books we find so interesting, the football match that is so exciting.

(R)

For those we trust to get us to school safely or to take us on our holidays.

(R)

And for those who are interested enough in us to give up time and leisure so that we can enjoy the fellowship of our clubs at church and school.

(R)

EXCITEMENT OF TRAVEL

Lord, how exciting it is to travel! Thank you for cars, aeroplanes, buses, trains and ships. Thank you for those whose expertise makes travel faster, safer, more comfortable. Thank you for those engaged in the exciting task of developing new forms of transport like hovercraft and space-ships.

Thank you for the interesting and exciting people we meet as we travel.

Thank you just for the fun of travel.

A TRAVELLER'S PRAYER

Help me, Lord, to know that wherever I travel in your world, I cannot travel outside your care.

Grant to those to whom I entrust myself, the pilot, the engine driver or the ship's captain, a clear mind, a steady hand, and the skills to do his job safely and well.

For in trusting myself to their care, I trust myself to you.

MIXING WITH THE OPPOSITE SEX

Lord, you have so made us that we cannot help but be interested in the other sex. Thank you for:

the fun we can have together,
the interests we can explore,
the secrets we can share.

Give to us:

a respect for each other,
patience with each other,
consideration for each other.

Help me to treat the other sex as people, not playthings. Grant that in my dealings with them I need never have cause for shame.

CONFESSION OF SELFISHNESS

The response is: **Lord Jesus, forgive us.**

Our Father, we confess that when we deal with other people we are not always at our best. The men and women who lead our youth groups give up so much of their spare time for us, and we take it all for granted.

(R)

We treat our youth club with far less respect than we treat our homes.

(R)

Nor do we give to our leaders the respect that is their due.

(R)

We would prefer it if some of the youngsters who belong to the club stayed away because we don't like them, or their dress, or their noise or their behaviour.

(R)

Indeed, Father, sometimes we reckon we would feel happier if we were the only members who came.

(R)

Help us to find among our companions and our leaders the fellowship which is a reflection of your love for us all.

'LOVE ONE ANOTHER'

Jesus said, 'Love one another as I have loved you'. This, Lord, is easy with some people –
    they have the same interests as I have;
    they speak the same language as I do;
    they behave in the same sort of way as I do.
It isn't so easy to love those who are different from me –
    those who don't like the games I enjoy;
    those who live in a different part of the town;
    those whose pattern of behaviour is different.
We remember though that it wasn't just his friends that Jesus loved. There was:
    the leper;
    the prostitute;
    the tax collector;
    the Roman soldier.
And more than those –
    the friends who let him down and deserted or
        betrayed him.
Jesus said, 'If you only love those who love you, what reward can you expect? Surely the tax gatherers do as much as that.'

But how can I love people I don't like? Help me Lord, to be caring towards them; to be interested in the boy who doesn't do as well as I do at school; to be considerate of the boy whose pattern of life I don't understand; to be patient with those who don't like doing what I want to do.

So Lord, help me to love others, whatever kind of people they happen to be.

WE ARE ALL DIFFERENT

How different, Lord, we all are! I sit at my examination desk and find no real difficulty in unravelling the problems of mathematics. But the intricacies of physics baffle me, and my mind goes blank when I look at the French paper. But John finds French as easy as I do maths, while Jim delights in untangling the physics. But Lord, there are many of my schoolmates who couldn't sit for these exams but have skills in woodwork, art, or games, that I wish I had. Lord, how different we all are!

It's the same in the youth club. Some only want to listen to records, while others want to do Bible study. Some want badminton or table tennis while others think time would be better spent in discussion.

In hobbies, clothes and music, we all have different tastes and interests. Give me tolerance, Lord, to accept others as I would want them to accept me.

Lord, how different we all are; how boring life would be if we were all the same! Thank you, Lord, for the great variety of life.

PRAYER FOR THE HANDICAPPED

Lord, we pray –

for the BLIND who see your light
but never the morning sun;
for the DEAF who hear your voice
but never the morning chorus;
for the MENTALLY HANDICAPPED who grasp your truth
but never the morning news.

PRACTICAL CONCERN

Four architects replanned a neighbourhood in a large city. They cared about the people who needed housing there. They listened to those people talking about their everyday needs – the particular needs caused by shift work, the need for protection from vandalism, the need to keep the community they knew in the old narrow streets.

The architects had their theories about how to build, but they modified them to suit these particular people. Their care had to express itself through many different administrative stages. Their completed work is a solid witness that caring counts, and caring can succeed.

O Jesus Christ, your concern is for all men. We pray for all who plan and build the homes we live in. We do not know the pressures of life they live with, but we do know how much other people's welfare depends upon people like them. Where such public service is offered may your Spirit inspire and your life replenish the sympathy and compassion they need.

FOR THOSE IN AUTHORITY

Jesus Christ, Lord of the whole world, give determination to politicians, trade unions, and management in building together a world more just than anything we have known.

Our part in that struggle as yet is small, and often the endless disputes of our elders test our patience. But, Lord, it would be fatal if we lost all confidence that the aim is worth the effort, the set-backs, and the rivalries.

Help us not to succumb to the temptation to personal peace and serenity, at the price of other people's lives and well-being.

The Worlds' Needy People.

LUKE 7 v 1 – 10

This message of Jonah –
that Gods love + mercy know
no limits

LEARNING FROM PEOPLE OF OTHER FAITHS

Jesus said, 'Go forth, and make all nations my disciples'. Lord, we thank you for missionaries, who at your call have carried the good news of Jesus to places far away – to Africa, India, the South Seas; to China and South America. But Lord, help us not to be arrogant as we talk about Jesus to people of other faiths. We know that Jesus is *the* way, *the* truth and *the* life; that he alone can disclose to us your fullness and that he said, 'No one comes to the Father but by me'. Yet, Lord, since he is the truth, all truth by which men live is his. While then, we seek to lead all the peoples of the world to him, help us not to forget the insights into truth that other faiths have to show us; nor to undervalue the heritage into which they have entered.

Make us always ready to learn even as we teach, and rightly to value truth wherever we find it.

IMMIGRANTS

'They' are always grumbling about immigrants! But I have learned such a lot from them!

They always seem to be so cheerful; their music is noisy, but they *enjoy* it; they have a smile – even when people ignore them. They have helped me to discover what an exciting world it is in which we live; for I have to learn something about strange countries; different religions; wonderful buildings; great rivers and high mountains.

They seem to have such a wonderful family life; wherever they go, the whole family seems to go – how they enjoy being together!

I can't understand them when they speak in their own language; I find some of the customs strange; I don't like the food they seem to enjoy. But, Lord, I enjoy being with them. And I know that you love them as much as you love me.

LIFE IN OTHER COUNTRIES

I wonder, Lord, what it must be like to live abroad. Hot, sunny summers; warm, relaxing winters; snowcapped mountains; crystal-clear rivers; sport and sunbathing and surf-riding.

But I wonder, Lord, whether this is the whole picture? Drought and famine and suffering and hardship? Lord, help those who need you in faraway places.

THE WORLD'S NEEDY PEOPLE

The response is: **Hear us, O Lord.**

Heavenly Father, you have created all men; they live in all sorts of places, and situations and conditions; for all the world's peoples we pray to you now:

For all the myriads of people who never have enough to eat.

(R)

For those who face discrimination because of their religion.

(R)

For those who are denied opportunities because of their colour.

(R)

For those who live in fear because of war, or revolution or insecurity.

(R)

For those boys and girls who will never grow up into manhood or womanhood because of disease.

(R)

Help us, O God, to be as concerned about other people as Jesus was.

10. People Who Help Us

OUR LOCAL GOVERNMENT COUNCIL

I take it for granted Lord, that there will be books for me to borrow from the library when I want them. I get mad when the bus is late coming in the morning and makes me late for school. The school is always there, and though sometimes it is a bind to have to go, I know that through its discipline and its training I am the better equipped for life.

I forget Lord, that there are a lot of people who are needed to provide me with the facilities I take for granted, and for them now I pray:

The councillors, who spend hours in committee deciding what can be done, and who in the end get lots of brickbats and few thanks.

The Chief Executive, the Finance Officer, the Chief Education Officer and the other officers of the Council who enable the services of the town to run smoothly.

The staff of the authority, bus drivers, teachers and refuse collectors, who do the jobs that we take for granted.

Thank you for them, Lord; help them to do their work well.

GOVERNMENT

Lord, we pray for our Queen. Sometimes we envy her. But we know that she must be lonely and isolated. She must long sometimes to do the ordinary things that ordinary people can do. She must long just to be herself. Lord, help her always to find in you the strength to set the sort of example that will enrich the life of the nation.

Lord, we pray for the government, those who are set in authority under her, that they may have wisdom to guide the nation in ways that lead to peace and happiness; that they may have compassion for those who are hardest hit by poverty or disablement or illness; and that they may have integrity to do what is right and honest without fear or favour.

A DIALOGUE: LEADING TO THANKS FOR DOCTORS AND NURSES

A. I hope I never have to go into hospital.

B. So do I. But I am glad that hospitals are there in case I need to go in one day.

C. I have been in hospital. There really is nothing to be afraid of.

B. I know that's true really. It's just the thought of being there, and being ill . . . .

A. And of doctors and nurses looking at you.

C. They are so kind. Even when they know they are going to have to hurt you, they give you such confidence.

A. I wondered whether I might be a doctor.

B. That's funny because I have always wanted to be a nurse. You've seen doctors and nurses at work; what do you think?

C. They've got to be kind people; somehow, though there are lots of people in a ward, they make you feel as if they are there just to help you to get better.

B. Is it hard work?

C. Sometimes the nurses look jolly tired. I suppose they have a right to be because they always seem to be walking around, doing this and doing that – they never seem to sit down and have a break.

A. But it must be wonderful to see people walk out of hospital when they had to be wheeled in on a trolley, and know that you have helped to make them better.

B. Just as it must have been for Jesus. What a thrill it must have been to him to hear a man speak, who had been dumb, and know that it was because he had done it.

A. I suppose that's true of doctors and nurses today. In a way they are just the hands that God uses to heal.

C. Thank God for doctors and nurses who put their skills and compassion at God's service, so that he can use them to bring healing.

CONFESSION

After each sentence, the response is: **Jesus, forgive.**

Lord, when I think of how much other people have to do to help me feel comfortable, I am ashamed –

That I grumble when the light won't go on, or that the cycle shop is shut when I want some spare part to repair my bicycle. **(R)**

That I take things like electricity and gas and water for granted and only think about them when they are not there. **(R)**

That I expect the doctor to be around quickly when I am ill and don't spare a thought for the millions of people who have to walk many miles even to see a doctor. **(R)**

That I forget to switch off the electric fire even when I no longer need it because I don't think of the danger the miner faces to dig the coal that runs some of the power stations. **(R)**

That I accept help from other people as my right and not as a privilege. **(R)**

Lord, help me not so much to be served as to serve.

'BEAR ONE ANOTHER'S BURDENS' *(Galatians 6. 2)*

I think of Jesus and of the man, Simon by name, who carried the heavy beam of the cross to Calvary for Jesus. He *had* to do it. The Roman soldiers conscripted him.

There are lots of people who carry burdens for me, not because they have to, nor because they get anything out of it, but just because they love me, or are interested in me, or because they want me to get the best out of life.

Lord, help them to carry the load they carry for me.

THOSE WHO TRAIN TEACHERS

Lord, I'm amazed at the range of skills and knowledge that my teachers have. But I'm sure they couldn't do their job as well as they do if they hadn't been trained for it. So, Lord, I want to pray for those who train people to teach:

For college principals, professors and lecturers.
It is a world so remote from my own narrow experience.
Lord, in their pursuit of truth, lead them to yourself, for you *are* the truth.
For the staff of universities and polytechnics.
We pray that they may never be so remote from the real world that they cannot effectively prepare those who teach in our world.

THOSE WHO WORK WITH THEIR HANDS

Lord Jesus, you were not ashamed to be known as a workman. Your hands got blistered with the tools of the carpenter. But you were able proudly to say, 'My yokes are easy'.

I pray, Lord, for all who work with their hands:

In car factories and cotton mills;
In the fields and on the railways;
In the home and office;
In studio and warehouse . . .

Lord, help them all to be workmen who have no need to be ashamed.

11. Pictures, Words and Music

THANKSGIVING FOR MEANS OF COMMUNICATION

(a)

After each sentence the response is: **Thank you, Lord, for the marvels of science.**

For TV sets that enable us to see things happening on the other side of the world, as they happen:

(R)

For newspapers that keep us up to date with the worlds of politics and sport:

(R)

For recorders and record-players, and the music we are able to enjoy:

(R)

For radio that helps us to feel involved in all that happens in the world:

(R)

For all those whose technical skill makes it possible for us to see and read and hear all that goes on in our wonderful world.

(R)

(b)

For poet's pen and writer's art;
For the genius of the musician and the insight of the artist;
For the wisdom of the sage and the courage of the prophet;
Lord our God, we thank you.

WAYS OF WORSHIP

Lord God, we use many ways in which to worship you.
We use books, whose words conjure up to us a picture of your love.
We use films, that we may see you working in our busy world.
We use recorders and record-players; we act and we dance.
We pray that through every part of our worship we may worthily praise you.

THE DISCOTHEQUE: A MEDITATION

It's exciting!
It's fabulous!
Music, movement, colour.
A confused jangle of noise and bodies.
But it does something to you.
It sets the feet tapping and your whole body wants to respond to the beat.
This is for real.

What is it, this place of music and colour and movement and noise?
My parents say they wouldn't be seen dead in the place.
Perhaps that's what appeals to me.
It's *ours*; our private world.
It's my music, my movement, my colour, my noise.
Nobody to scream, 'Turn that thing down ! ! !'
It's what I like, what expresses me.
Here I can relax and have my fun, and go back refreshed to the tasks and duties of life.

For I must be careful.
This is not all that living is about.
Jesus spoke about real life. He said,
'I have come that men may have life, and may have it in all its fullness'.
Lord, that's the life I want.
I love the discotheque.
But thank you for Jesus.

A DIALOGUE ON NEWSPAPERS: INTRODUCTION TO PRAYER

A. I always turn to the back page first.

B. I suppose that's because that's the sports page. As if sport was the most important thing in life!

A. Well, isn't it? Who wants to be bothered about fashion and letters to the Editor, and all that nonsense?

B. There's more to newspapers than that – what about the front page with its headlines about the great events that are changing our world?

A. That's only about bombs and bullets, and revolutions – hooligans and vandals tearing the world apart. Who's interested in that?

B. You ought to be. It's your world and you ought to know what's going on in it.

A. You only find out from the newspapers what they want you to know. News with a slant. Papers with an axe to grind. That's newspapers today.

B. Maybe with some, yes. But if you took the trouble to read, you would get at the facts. Your trouble is that you are not interested!

A. What did you mean just now by saying that it was my world. I thought you always reckoned that it was God's world. Make up your mind one way or the other.

B. It is your world in the sense that you live it and are responsible for what happens in that part of it which is your preserve. But it is God who is King.

A. Does that mean that it doesn't matter what happens in the capital cities of the world – the headlines you talked about, about the great events that are changing our world?

B. Of course it matters. But what we believe is that there is greater news than that – good news – that God loved our world so much that Jesus came to rescue it. Maybe if we could read good news like that in our newspapers, our world might become a different place.

USING GOD'S GIFTS

Lord God, my grandparents tell me about life when there was no record-player and no television. I can't really imagine what it must have been like, Lord. But I see that it must have been a different sort of life, and that some of the changes have not been wholly good.

It is so easy Lord, just to sit in front of the television set and be spectators, without ever getting really involved in anything. It is so easy, Lord, to let other people entertain us and to lose all the skills of music-making; the enjoyment of reading; the stimulus of conversation and discussion. It is so easy, Lord, to imagine that the world of the TV screen is the real world and to slip into the standards of that world without questioning them. It is so easy, Lord, to be satisfied with the mediocre and forget there is a higher and a better way calling us. And it is so easy, Lord, in the enjoyment we get to forget that there are duties of life we are shirking and tasks that somebody else has to undertake for us.

Lord, I thank you for TV and record-players and the other gadgetry of our technological world. But help me not to be enslaved by them.

BEING GOT AT

Lord, I have the feeling all the time that they are getting at me.

The adverts on TV.
The jingles on radio.
The headlines in the papers.
The hoardings.
The films.

I know, Lord, that I am a target of the media, that it's me they're after. I suppose, Lord, that makes me important. But I don't want to be used by the manipulators. I want to enjoy life and to be myself.

Lord, help me to read and listen with discernment and not to be led into doing foolish things.

THE INFLUENCERS

Lord, we can't shut our ears or our eyes to the torrent of words that are hurled at us every day on radio and TV, in newspapers and magazines. Help us to listen and to react with discrimination and judgement. Hear us as we pray for those who are able, by compelling words, to influence the peoples of our world:

We pray, Lord, for authors and journalists, that their skill with words may be used to uphold the best of values and not to glamorise the sordid. *(Pause)*

We pray, Lord, for editors and sub-editors, that their selection of news and headlines may not distort truth but give a right balance. *(Pause)*

We pray, Lord, for writers of plays and scripts for comedy, that they may uphold high standards of values. *(Pause)*

Lord, we thank you for all these people. Help and guide them in their responsible jobs.

MUSIC

Lord, music reflects every mood and every experience of man. People express their worship through music. Sometimes its cadences bring comfort in life's tragic experiences. It reflects our moods of gaiety and romance. Lord, thank you for the ability to make music and for being able to express my many moods in the music I make or that I listen to.

Be always the inspiration of those who compose music. Through those who play, bring enjoyment, inspiration and consolation to those who listen.

FILMS

Lord, I love watching films – comedies, westerns, murders, musicals, horror films – the lot. I can't say I enjoy watching all of them. Some make me curl up inside in horror and fear. Some reflect a world that isn't real and others exalt values I don't accept. But others are pure enjoyment and fun – I find myself letting go as I watch them.

Lord, help me to be able to appreciate the good and reject the bad. Help those then who make films and act in them, that they might never forget how easily some people succumb to evil. Make them sensitive, Lord to the power they exert over the minds of men and women.

BOOKS AND READING

(a)

Big books and paperbacks;
novels and histories and plays;
romance and tragedy;
cartoons and picture books;
serious and gay;
borrowed and bought;
books and comics.

Thank you, God, for books and the gift of reading.

(b)

For all great literature we praise you, O God:
for fine poetry,
for pictures painted in words,
for stories, novels, biographies, histories,
for the skilful work of the playwright.
For writers and their writings, enriching the life of man.
We give you praise, O God.

12. Special Events

THE NEW YEAR

(a)

There's something special, Father, about a new year.
It's as though we stand on a threshold.
We can look both ways –
back to the past, finished and fixed;
forward to the future, unknown and mysterious.

Here and now, Father, at the turn of the year,
we commit ourselves to your love and goodness
which has kept us in the past
and will never let us go.

(b)

We thank you, O God, for all your good gifts to us in the year that is ending:
for our homes, our families, our friends,
for school, club, games and hobbies;
for the special occasions that meant so much,
for the everyday things we took for granted;
but most of all for your presence always with us.

(c)

Father, we have come to the end of one year and the beginning of another. We know that during the past year we have not always been the people we should have been: we have thought so much about ourselves, and so little about you and other people.

But we also know that your love revealed in Jesus forgives and makes everything new. We gladly accept your forgiveness, Father, and ask you to give us a new start in a new year.

HARVEST

(a)

At this harvest-time, let's remind ourselves of God's goodness in creating us; in providing for our daily needs. In silence we offer our praise and thanks. *(Silence)* As we gives thanks for God's love, we remember our own failure to love.

Lord, you have shown us unfailing love, and we have not loved enough in return; you have given and given again, and we take your gifts for granted. Forgive us for pleasing ourselves rather than pleasing you, for thinking so much of our own needs and so little about other people's. Help us to show our thanks for all your goodness by the way we live our lives.

(b)

Thank you, Lord,
for all the harvest of the land –
for corn, vegetables, fruit, flowers.

Thank you
for the harvest of the earth –
for oil, coal, salt, water.

Thank you
for the harvest of the sea –
for creatures and fish of many kinds.

Thank you
for those people who help to supply our needs,
for farmers and fishermen, and workers in industry.

Teach us to remember, Lord, how much we depend on you, and how much we depend on others.

(c)

What does harvest festival mean to us?
It means plenty of everything –
food to eat, coal to burn,
flowers to display, clothes to wear.
We never go short. We celebrate our plenty.

But very many people in the world
have little or no harvest:
little or nothing to eat or drink,
no new clothes, nowhere to live.
Nothing to celebrate.

Father, grant that the harvest will mean for us
not just a celebration by us who 'have',
but a real concern for all who 'have not'.
May your Spirit move us, and men everywhere,
to work for the relief of our needy brothers and sisters.

REMEMBRANCE

Almost every day, Father, we see in the news accounts of war and violence. When will the world learn the lessons of the past?

On this day, Father, when we remember those whose lives were lost through war, we ask that you will teach the whole world, and us, to live not by violence but in peace, not by hatred but in love.

CHURCH ANNIVERSARY

Lord God, as we look back over the last year in the life of this church, we give you our thanks:
for the members of our church, and their loyalty to it;
for the worship regularly offered;
for the activities that exist for young and old;
for the faithful work of our minister and leaders;
for what our church has achieved in our neighbourhood, especially amongst people in need.

Lord God, as we look forward to the coming year, once again we offer our church, and ourselves, to you. May your Spirit strengthen our faith and increase our love.

THE BEGINNING OF TERM (YEAR)

(a)

The response is: **In the name of Jesus Christ.**

As this new term (year) begins, we pray for our school, that all who teach, all who learn, all who care for our needs, may work together for the good of all. Lord, we offer this prayer . . .

(R)

We pray for our work during the term (year), that in it we may serve you with all our minds. Lord, we offer this prayer . . .

(R)

We pray for our games and recreations, that in them we may learn to be fair, generous and unselfish. Lord, we offer this prayer . . .

(R)

Lord, as we begin this term (year), we pledge ourselves to the ideal of love. Help us to love you by making the most of what we are and by giving the best we have; and help us to love others by giving ourselves to their service.

Two prayers – (b) and (c) – written by young people

(b)

Lord, during this term help us to be thoughtful towards those around us, to sympathise when they are in trouble, to go through this new term with unselfishness and good intentions.

Help us as we make a fresh start. May we work hard and play fair. May we come closer to you, Lord.

(c)

At the beginning of this term, Father, teach us to think of others as well as ourselves. Help us so that mistakes we made before with people, we may not make again. Make us kind to our schoolmates, even the ones we don't like.

Thank you for the friendship of companions, and the help of our teachers. Thank you for the love of our Lord, Jesus Christ.

THE SCHOOL DAY

A prayer written by a teenager

Lord, as we go about our daily duties,
help us to think of those who work for us:
 the teachers with all their responsibilities,
 the cleaners who tidy up after us,
 the cooks who prepare our meals,
 the people who wash our plates after we have eaten.
Help us to think especially of you –
 you who help, guide and protect us all through the day.

END OF THE SCHOOL TERM (YEAR)

As we come to the end of this term (year), let's remember in silence some of those things that have meant most to us here, and let us be thankful for them. *(Silence)*
Lord God, we are grateful
 for all that life offers us,
 for all that we have known in this place,
 for the people we have met,
 for the experiences that have helped us to grow and develop,
 for learning and leisure,
 for the opportunity to contribute to the common good,
 for all that we have learned of beauty, truth and goodness.
May gratitude for all these gifts inspire us to live lives of humility, and of service.

HOLIDAYS

(a)

Lord, as we (end this term and) begin the holidays,
we thank you
for opportunities for rest and recreation,
for occasions to look forward to,
for the change to a different routine.

Help us, Lord, during these holidays
to use our time wisely,
to have time for other people, and
to honour you in everything we do.

(b)

Lord, we thank you for the holidays and the change they bring:
the chance of a lie-in in the morning,
the more leisurely pace we live at,
listening to records or the radio,
time to stand and stare,
time to appreciate sea, hills, countryside, rivers, trees,
time to give to other people – our families, friends, people who need help.
Lord, we thank you for the holidays.
May the change refresh and renew us.

THANKS FOR PARTIES

We thank you, Father, for the pleasure there is in a party:
for the special occasion we are celebrating,
for the relaxed atmosphere,
for the fun and laughter,
for the food specially prepared,
for the chance to mix with friends.
In all our enjoyment, help us, Father, to be considerate towards others, and thankful to you.

BIRTHDAY

They say that if you're sad on your birthday, you'll be miserable for forty days after it! I don't believe that, Lord. But I do believe that a birthday should be a happy day.

For one thing, it's a day for giving thanks, thanks to relations and friends for all they have done for me during the year, and for their good wishes for the future; thanks to you, Lord, for this milestone in my life, for bringing me safely through another year.

And it's a day to start afresh, to look ahead and step out on a new year, to resolve to be a better follower of Jesus.

Help me, Lord, as I enter on another stage of my life.

CELEBRATIONS

From time to time, Father, we all have something to celebrate – a special day, a piece of good news, or a member of the family coming home after a long time away. Or perhaps our favourite team wins an important game, or we ourselves do well at sport, or pass an exam.

Whenever we do celebrate a big occasion, teach us, Father, to be grateful for the joy it brings, and to remember those who have nothing to celebrate.

13. Opening and Closing Prayers

OPENING PRAYERS

(a)

To you, O God, Father, Son and Holy Spirit,
all creation offers its praise –
  the earth and the sky,
  the mountains and hills,
  creatures of sea and land and air,
  the life and skills of mankind.
Accept our praises too.

(b)

Lord, when the Psalmist wanted to worship you, he just looked out upon the world and sang his praises. Just as the heavens tell out your glory, we want to sing of your love. Lord, help us to worship you now.

(c)

'I was glad when they said to me, "Let us go to the house of the Lord."' Grant us, Father, the right frame of mind for worship, that we may be aware of your power and goodness, and be willing and eager to serve you.

(d)

Father, you have called us into the fellowship of your Church. Make us worthy of our calling.

(e)

Paul said, 'I appeal to you therefore, brethren, by the mercies of God, to present your bodies as a living sacrifice, holy and acceptable to God which is your spiritual worship.'

Lord, we will use many words in our worship. We will also make music. Help us, in dance and rhythm and mime, to use our bodies to express our worship to you.

(f)

Lord, you spoke, and the worlds came into being. Grant that through every word we shall hear today, we may feel your creative power.

(g)

For every new beginning, God's name be praised: beginnings provided by the calendar, or happenings in the home, or new starts in school or club. For the opportunities which these times offer us to make new resolutions, God's name be praised.

(h)

Glory to God in the highest and now also upon earth. We praise you, we bless you, we glorify your name, now and always.

CLOSING PRAYERS

(a)

Your Spirit, Lord, filled the early Church with enthusiasm, boldness and a sense of adventure. May we also find in our worship, and in our work for you, that same sense of challenge and excitement.

(b)

Father, may our light so shine before men, that they may see the good we do, and offer praise to you.

(c)

Thank you, God, for the Church. Thank you for its existence, for all the good it has achieved, and for its witness to our Lord Jesus Christ. Help us, in our lives, to be worthy of it.

(d)

Lord Jesus, we offer our hands to work for you, and our mouths to speak for you, in the world today.

(e)

Lord, you spoke of a city on a hill that could not be hidden. You spoke of men seeing good works and praising you for them. May our lives and our behaviour bring you praise and glory.

(f)

Lord, we offer ourselves as a living sacrifice, holy, a wholehearted service to you.

(g)

You send us out as the apostles were sent out, Lord Jesus. As you showed them, show us also, we ask, the precise commission we must fulfil.

(h)

In your glory, love and power, O God, we confidently put our trust.

(i)

'You will know them by their fruits,' Jesus said. That applies to all of us. Father, may our lives bear the fruit of your Spirit's presence, that people may see that we are followers of Jesus.

(j)

O Holy Spirit, may the breath of your life and the fire of your love be found in us.

(k)

Send us out, Lord, in the strength of your Spirit, to think, speak and act to your glory.

INDEX